Restoring American Manufacturing

A Practical Guide

David P. Goldman

Washington Fellow
The Claremont Institute's CENTER FOR THE AMERICAN WAY OF LIFE

PROVOCATIONS #5
CLAREMONT INSTITUTE
CENTER FOR THE AMERICAN WAY OF LIFE

Design: **David Reaboi**/Strategic Improvisation

Published in the United States by the Claremont Institute

CLAREMONT
PRESS

RESTORING AMERICAN MANUFACTURING

A Practical Guide

Whenever the federal government spends a dollar, demons awake and go abroad to encourage rent-seeking and cronyism. Industrial policy of the sort practiced by European social democracies has become a dirty word, and with good reason. Humanity has not discovered a worse or more corruption-prone mechanism for misallocating resources than committees of civil servants appointed by politicians. Nonetheless, every developed economy has an industrial policy of sorts, embedded in its tax, regulatory, public works, and other policies.

America already has a massive, pervasive, and comprehensive industrial policy, but a policy so perverse that it has hollowed out America's industrial economy and suppressed the incomes and capabilities of American workers. The federal government has an enormous influence on the allocation of capital among different sectors of the economy. For example:

1

- The American tax code favors "capital light" Big Tech companies and penalizes capital-intensive manufacturing.

- American regulation, including environmental and worker safety regulation, favors companies with a preponderance of white-collar employees at the expense of manufacturing, mining, chemical, and refining industries.

- The United States provides enormous subsidies to universities through tax-exempt status and direct grants, favoring elite universities with large endowments and research facilities, taxing average Americans to fund the education of elite professionals. Other countries subsidize apprenticeship programs for less-affluent citizens to train a highly skilled and highly paid industrial workforce.

- The United States spends just 0.55 percent of GDP annually on infrastructure, about the same level as Greece, compared to 0.8 percent in Germany, 0.9 percent in France, 1.1 percent in Japan and 5.8 percent in China. Public improvements are a subsidy to goods-producing industry and mining, and America's level of spending is among the lowest in the industrial world.

- Federal subsidies for R&D subsidize innovative, entrepreneurial industries. During the 1970s and 1980s, the federal R&D budget was about 1 percent of GDP, and federal funding supported every invention of the Digital Age, helping to make America the world's undisputed leader in advanced technology. Today, the federal R&D budget is only 0.3 percent of GDP.

- The largest discretionary component of federal spending, the $1.75 trillion Department of Defense allocation, includes vast payments to industries. At

2

the peak of the Cold War during the late 1970s and the 1980s, defense policy demanded a wide range of innovations in weapons systems that required the discovery of new technologies. These new technologies were adopted by entrepreneurs who created new industries in computation, communications, materials science, and other fields. Today the defense acquisitions budget supports a small group of giant defense contractors who have little incentive to innovate.

Whether most Americans realize it or not, we have an industrial policy that discourages capital-intensive investment through taxation and regulation, subsidizes the education of white-collar professionals rather than skilled workers and engineers, neglects infrastructure, and skimps on the kind of scientific research that translates into industrial productivity.

But we also have an industrial policy by omission. The absence of a policy is also a policy when the competition has a policy. Our strategic rival China spends over 1.7 percent of GDP in direct subsidies to favored domestic industries, according to a study by the Center for Strategic and International Studies.[1] China also provides indirect subsidies to key industries. A 2019 study by *The Wall Street Journal* estimated that Huawei Technologies had received approximately $75 billion in state support over the past twenty-five years, including $25 billion in tax incentives and $46 billion in loans on favorable terms from state lenders.[2] The numbers may be overstated (by counting the full value of a loan as a subsidy), but it is clear that Huawei enjoyed the full backing of the Chinese government. In the United States, by contrast, the Trump Administration in 2017 rejected a proposal to provide federal support for 5G broadband by a National Security Council Strategist, General Robert Spalding.

FIGURE 1. US MERCHENDISE TRADE BALANCE

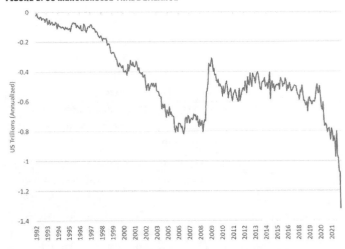

FIGURE 2. STOCKS DOMINATE FOREIGN INVESTMENT IN US SECURITIES

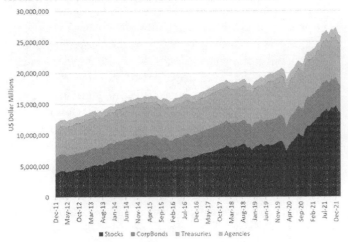

China not only has 70 percent of the world's installed 5G capacity as well as thousands of private-network applications to ports, warehouses, and factories. It is also exporting 5G systems to countries as diverse as Indonesia, Brazil, Mexico, and the United Arab Emirates.

THE CONSEQUENCES OF BAD INDUSTRIAL POLICY

The result of our perverse industrial policy is falling real incomes, dependence on foreign suppliers (notably China) and rapidly accumulating foreign debt. During the past thirty years, from 1992 through May of 2022, America's trade balance on goods was a cumulative negative $18 trillion. That is exactly equal to America's net foreign investment position, also $18 trillion. We have exchanged $18 trillion worth of Treasury bonds, corporate stocks, real estate, and other assets, for $18 trillion worth of goods. The rate at which we must sell assets to buy goods is accelerating. During 2022 our trade deficit on goods exceeded $100 billion in every month from January to May.

America's soaring trade deficit, now running at a record $1.32 trillion annual rate, requires the United States to sell paper to its foreign suppliers in return for goods. Most of the paper the United States sold to foreigners during the past few years was equity in US corporations, rather than government or corporate bonds. Valuations in the US stock market soared as the Federal Reserve forced interest rates lower, by reducing its short-term lending rate to zero and by purchasing $6 trillion of Treasury securities. (See FIG 1.)

The result of this exercise is the worst inflation in forty years and a collapse of labor productivity that portends shrinking corporate profits. With a net foreign asset position of $18 trillion, the United States cannot go on selling its assets to foreigners indefinitely. At some point, the orderly sale of US assets might turn into a fire sale. (FIG 2.)

Foreign holdings of US stocks jumped from $8.5 trillion in early 2020 to $13.5 trillion today, while foreign ownership of US Treasuries barely increased. The Fed, that is, bought $6 trillion in Treasuries, real yields collapsed, and equity valuations soared. Foreigners shunned record low yields on US government paper and bought into the equity boom.

What if foreigners stop buying US equities? Several things can happen (and all of them probably will). First, the United States will have to sell more bonds to foreigners, and at more attractive yields. That means real yields will have to rise even further, putting more pressure on equity valuations. Secondly, foreigners will cut the price at which they buy US assets—that is, the dollar will have to fall. Third, Americans will buy fewer foreign goods, which means that demand will fall. That's another name for a recession.

WHAT KIND OF INDUSTRIAL POLICY DO WE NEED?

We have underinvested in capital and failed to train labor. We invest less in industry than we did before the COVID-19 pandemic. We are short of capital and short of qualified labor. One million manufacturing jobs were advertised in May 2022 that could not find applicants, and the shortfall in factory workers is likely to double during this decade.

As noted, our perverse industrial policy is comprehensive and embedded in every sphere of government activity—taxation, regulation, infrastructure, education, and defense. Reversing our industrial decline requires comprehensive reforms. There is a temptation to find a simple solution—for example, a tariff on imports from China. As noted below, our imports from China before the Trump administration's tariffs went into effect ran at a $410 billion annual rate. As of May our imports from China ran at a nearly $700 billion annual rate, an increase of more than half.

We should remember H. L. Mencken's quip: "For every complex problem, there's a solution that is simple, neat and wrong." But there is a guiding principle that is simple and clear, although working out its details will be complicated: We have to build the industries of the future rather than attempt to revive the industries of the past.

Here, in summary, is what we must do if we want to remain a world manufacturing power:

1. Start by recognizing that it's worse than we thought and later than we think. China continues to gain on the United States in manufacturing, with a single-minded plan to dominate the next generation of industrial technology. China invests more capital and trains more engineers than we do. We cannot decouple from China. But we can slow the rate of increase of our dependency on China and begin to reverse it over time.

2. Pick our spots carefully. Our manufacturing capacity is too weak to try to do everything at once. Foster new industries at the cutting edge of technology rather than try to restore old ones, except in the case of strategically critical industries like semiconductors, advanced materials, special chemicals, pharmaceuticals, robotics, and telecommunications infrastructure.

3. Use the defense budget as a lever for technological transformation, on the model of the war-winning strategy of the 1970s and 1980s. Defense-related development spending shrank from about 1 percent of GDP in the early 1980s to about 0.3 percent of GDP at present, as defense spending shifted to purchases of legacy systems rather than innovation to create new ones. Defending the homeland

against the next generation of strategy weapons requires fundamental innovations in physics and computation, and it requires solving problems that will have a transformative impact on the civilian economy.

4. Target points of entry for new manufacturing companies that have immediate economic benefit and profit opportunities, including: flexible manufacturing for high-tech components; and new materials that have both civilian and military applications. We still dominate key niches, including specialty glass. Dominate more of them.

5. Train workers on the German model. The National Association of Manufacturers warns that the United States is short 2.1 million factory workers, and other estimates are even higher.[3] Create apprenticeship programs at the state level in partnership with state-supported community colleges to train workers in state-of-the-art robotics and other new industrial processes.

6. Train more engineers and scientists. China graduates six times as many engineers and computer scientists as we do. Revive the National Defense Education Act of 1958 to support scientific and technical education.

7. Revise immigration policy to favor highly qualified immigrants only. Many of China's and Russia's best engineers would relocate to the United States if given the opportunity.

8. Phase in domestic content requirements for military procurements and industries that receive federal subsidies, including civilian aircraft. Boeing's shift to outsourcing is a case history in deindustrialization. Force major US manufacturers to take

the initiative to incubate domestic suppliers. Most other industrialized nation do this.

9. Create financial incentives for pension funds and individuals to invest in stocks that serve national priorities, and allow US corporations to qualify for these incentives by serving national goals.

10. Create many public-private partnerships to subsidize basic research, while leaving the risk of commercialization to private investors.

What are the objections to industrial policy, and what merit do they have? It is true that the world is shifting away from hardware to software and the reduction of manufacturing in GDP is a natural result of technological progress. The US software industry, however, is overwhelmingly oriented toward consumer businesses and entertainment. Does not the free market make better investment decisions than the government? Yes, but with a qualification. Technological innovation should be motivated by the desire to improve ordinary life. But in practice, the requirements of war have driven innovation. The Second World War gave us nuclear power, computation, radar, and missiles that later made possible space travel. The Cold War gave us cheap and powerful computer chips, electronic displays, optical networks, GUI, the internet, and every other component of the digital age.

CHINA IS GAINING ON THE UNITED STATES

In August 2019, then-President Donald Trump imposed a 25 percent tariff on a wide range of Chinese goods. At a seasonally adjusted annual rate, China's exports to the United States stood at $407 billion. By March of 2022 they had risen to $675 billion, an increase of more than 60 percent. (FIG 3.)

FIGURE 3. CHINA EXPORT TO UNITED STATES

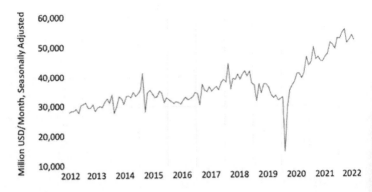

FIGURE 4. CᴀᴘEx PLANS FOR CHINA BIG TECH: MEDIAN +30% YoY (DEFLATED BY MANUFACTURING PPI)

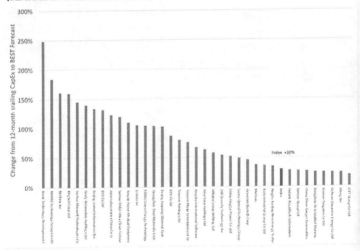

China's share of world manufacturing has grown rapidly since Trump's executive order took effect. China continues to pour investments into high-tech manufacturing with the aim of dominating the Fourth Industrial Revolution, that is, the application of artificial intelligence to manufacturing, logistics, urban management, medical care, and virtually every aspect of economic life.

The US trade deficit doubled. The combined $6 trillion stimulus to US consumption provided by the Trump and Biden administrations in response to the COVID pandemic meanwhile led to a doubling of the US trade deficit.

A prominent adviser to the Chinese government, Peking University economist Justin Yifu Lin, argued in a 2021 book that China must lead the Fourth Industrial Revolution.[4] Dr. Lin, a former chief economist of the World Bank and a University of Chicago PhD, wrote:

> Based on market exchange rates, China's economic scale has now reached 70% of the US. China's 5G technology has become the world leader in the new industrial revolution. In the past few years, the US has repeated its old tricks and suppressed Chinese companies with groundless accusations, using all of its national resources. If the US succeeds in suppressing China by means of a blockade in the new industrial revolution, China will not be able to achieve its second centennial goal.
>
> How can China break through the US blockade? It can only do this by working hard to lead the new industrial revolution. Then it will not be blocked, but will reach the technological level of the United States in its developed provinces, and achieve a national per capita GDP equal to half of that of the US by 2049. Therefore, it is a necessity for China to lead the new industrial revolution in order to achieve its second centennial goal by 2049.

China's investment in high-tech infrastructure includes the construction of 70 percent of the world's 5G broad-

FIGURE 5. US TECH 125 CaPEx +12% (DEFLATED BY INVESTMENT GOODS PPI)

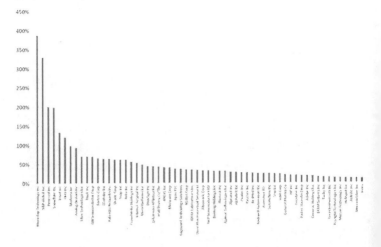

FIGURE 6. CAPITAL GOODS ORDERS REMAIN BELOW EARLIER PEAKS IN REAL TERMS

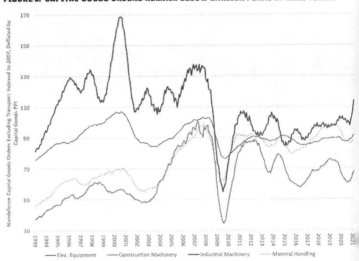

band capacity, the enabler of a new generation of technologies including fully automated ports, already-functioning autonomous taxi services, self-programming industrial robots, and the Internet of Things, which makes it possible for robots to track, sort, and expedite goods from factory to warehouse to ship, and then from ship to port to final customer.

A useful gauge of China's pace of high-tech investment is the capital spending of its largest tech companies (in this example, the members of the MSCI China Tech 100 Index). Shown in the chart above is the projected increase in the spending plans of China's largest tech firms (the difference between trailing twelve-month capital expenditures and the consensus analyst forecast for the next twelve months). The index as a whole is expected to show a 35 percent year-on-year increase in CapEx, adjusted to 30 percent after taking into account 4.8 percent producer price inflation for manufactured goods. (FIG. 4.)

By contrast, the companies in the MSCI US Tech 125 Index are expected to invest 12 percent more in the coming year than in the preceding year (after deducting 12 percent inflation in the investment goods component of the Producer Price Index). (FIG. 5.)

Not only Chinese companies, but Western companies are increasing investment in China faster than they are at home. A March 2022 report by the Peterson Institute for International Economics noted: "Despite years of calls by some Western governments for reshoring—relocating foreign investments away from China—and widespread commentary that deglobalization is the new trend, China's inbound foreign direct investment (FDI) in 2021 rose by a third to reach $334 billion, a new all-time high. The jump in FDI is documented in the 2021 Balance of Payments report published by the State Administration of Foreign Exchange of China."[5]

Investment in capital goods produced in the United States remains well below previous peaks. (FIG. 6.) Another gauge of manufacturing investment, the total capital expenditures of the sixty companies in the S&P 500 Industrials Sub-Index, remains depressed. In 2022, total CapEx by this group of major industrial companies will be 25 percent below its 2018 peak, and will recover only slightly during 2023, according to the consensus forecast of analysts surveyed by Bloomberg.

While global companies increased their investment in China by a third last year, they showed little interest in reshoring production to the United States or other venues outside the Chinese sphere. Morgan Stanley asked its industry analysts to survey the companies they cover to assess attitudes toward shifting supply chains out of China. The investment bank made this statement in a May research report:

> Analysts believe it is important for their industries to make investments to secure supply chains, with 42% of analysts believing these changes need to happen "fast" or "fastest." Despite this urgent need, company management teams do not seem receptive to making major supply chain changes and 58% of analysts rated these teams as "not receptive at all" or "somewhat unreceptive." Only 4% of North American management teams were rated as being highly receptive to making major changes vs. 7% in Europe and 21% in APAC.[6]

Virtually all the corporations polled by Morgan Stanley expected pressure on margins from reshoring owing to higher capital costs. Thirty-one percent said they would be able to pass on the higher cost of capital; 27 percent sai that higher capital costs would reduce profits; and 42 percent said that the result would be some combination of the two. That is, 69 percent of respondents believed that higher capital costs because of reshoring would wholly or partly reduce profit margins.

Any substantial expansion of capital investment in the United States would require an increase of imports, including imports from China, of tools and machinery. In 2021, American imports of capital goods rose to the level of US production of capital goods for domestic consumption (total capital goods production minus exports). That is, the United States now depends on imports for half its total consumption of capital goods. In order to eventually reduce dependence on China, the United States would first have to increase its dependence on China. (FIG. 7.)

The $6 trillion demand stimulus provoked the highest US inflation in forty years. This has eroded corporate profit margins, reflected in the nearly 20 percent decline in the S&P 500 Index in 2020 through May 19. US manufacturers have sharply reduced plans for capital investment, according to the Philadelphia Federal Reserve's monthly industrial survey.

Underinvestment in America's capital stock helps explain why productivity growth is the lowest on record. The long-term trend has been declining since the late 1990s, when the United States lost manufacturing jobs at the fastest pace on record. (FIG. 8.)

Productivity during the first quarter of 2022 declined at an annual rate of 7.5 percent, the worst quarter since 1947.

In summary:

1. America's export dependence on China has increased sharply during the past three years.

2. Western companies' commitment to China has risen sharply.

3. Corporate management pays lip service to the concept of shifting supply chains to the United States but has little intention of taking action that might reduce profit margins.

FIGURE 7. CAPGOODS IMPORTS NOW EXCEED
US PRODUCTION FOR DOMESTIC USE

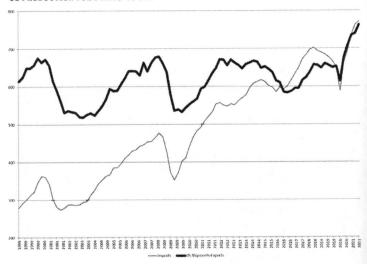

FIGURE 8. OUTPUT PER HOUR, 10-YEAR MOVING AVERAGE

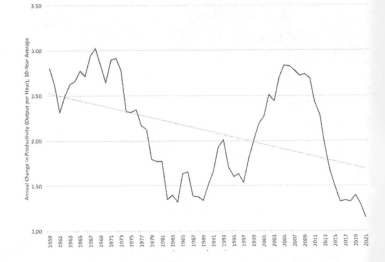

4. American productivity growth has been stagnant for a decade and appears to be in decline.

Alarm bells should be going off. What, then, can be done?

REDUCE THE COST OF CAPITAL FOR MANUFACTURING

In the spring of 2020, a senior executive of Huawei Technologies, the world's largest manufacturer of telecommunications infrastructure, asked the author why the United States had not arranged for Cisco Systems to buy Huawei's Swedish competitor Ericsson to create a "national champion" that could challenge Huawei. *The Wall Street Journal* reported on June 20, 2020:

> Cisco Chief Executive Chuck Robbins discussed a potential deal to buy all or part of a European equipment firm last year with [Lawrence] Kudlow, the White House economic adviser, though the talks were "more patriotism-driven" than a reflection of Cisco's merger interest, a person familiar with the meeting said. Mr. Robbins "didn't want the U.S. to fall behind," the person said, but the company, which makes computer networking gear, was unwilling to invest in a less profitable business like Nokia or Ericsson without some sort of financial incentives, the person added.[7]

Ericsson's profit margin currently is 9.45 percent, while Cisco's is 23.3 percent. Ericsson's return on equity has stayed in single digits, while Cisco's return on equity has been 30 percent to 40 percent in recent years. That raises the question: Why is Ericsson still in business? The answer is that its Swedish stockholders view it as a long-term investment of importance for Sweden's economic future and are willing to accept lower returns on their capital.

American capital markets, by contrast, funnel investments into enterprises that meet their criteria for risk-ad-

FIGURE 9. WEIGHTED AVERAGE COST OF CAPITAL: S&P INDUSTRIALS VS INFOTECH

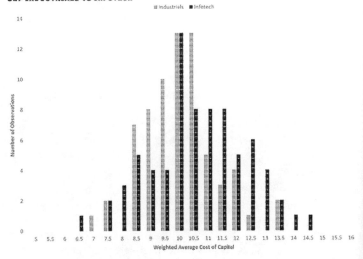

FIGURE 10. CAPITAL INTENSITY (TOTAL ASSETS/EARNINGS BEFORE INTEREST AND TAXES)

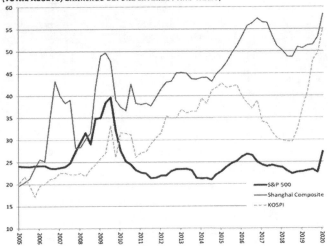

justed returns. The Weighted Average Cost of Capital among the seventy-five S&P 500 constituent companies classified as "information technology" is not much different than the WACC of the seventy-one constituents classified as "industrials." Weighted Average Cost of Capital is the rate of return that a company must pay investors for financing in the form of debt and equity. It is not surprising that industrial companies pay the same cost of capital as information technology companies; if they offered a lower return, the market would allocate capital elsewhere. (FIG. 9.)

The problem is that a vast shift of revenues and market capitalization has occurred during the past twenty years, away from goods-producing industries to consumer-oriented technology businesses that provide entertainment, computer services, shopping, and advertising services.

The market capitalization of the seventy-five constituents of the S&P 500 Industrials subindex as of August 8, 2022, was $3.25 trillion. By contrast, the combined market capitalization of the top six US information technology companies was $8.28 trillion.

The return on equity of the S&P Industrials subindex was 20 percent. The average return on equity of the six tech giants was 54 percent, and the ROE of the six companies ranged from 29 percent to 147 percent.

COMPANY	RETURN ON EQUITY
Apple	147
Microsoft	47
Netflix	38
Google	32
Meta	31
Amazon	29
Average	54
S&P Industrials	20

The United States has allowed the tech giants to build monopoly businesses than can exact extremely high rates of return. A 2020 report by the US Congressional Subcommittee on Antitrust warned:

> To put it simply, companies that once were scrappy, under-dog startups that challenged the status quo have become the kinds of monopolies we last saw in the era of oil barons and railroad tycoons. Although these firms have delivered clear benefits to society, the dominance of Amazon, Apple, Facebook, and Google has come at a price. These firms typically run the marketplace while also competing in it—a position that enables them to write one set of rules for others, while they play by another, or to engage in a form of their own private quasi regulation that is unaccountable to anyone but themselves.[8]

The monopoly position of the information technology industry creates a vast capital sink that draws investor funds into efforts to create new monopolies on the model of Amazon, Apple, Microsoft, and Google. This, in turn, has forced US industrial companies to minimize costs by shifting facilities overseas, outsource a large part of their production, and reduce the scale of their operations. US manufacturing employment has fallen from a peak of 19.5 million in 1989 to 12.5 million today.

By one key measure—the capital intensity of business operations—the American stock market has diverged from Asian markets. "Capital intensity is the amount of fixed or real capital," essentially tools and machinery, "present in relation to other factors of production, especially labor."[9] Shown in the chart below is the capital intensity of the S&P 500 compared to the Shanghai Composite Index, China's broadest index, and the Korean Stock Exchange Index (KOSPI). (FIG. 10.)

The capital intensity of listed Korean and Chinese companies doubled between 2005 and 2020 as those economies shifted toward manufacturing while the capital intensity of the S&P 500 remained unchanged.

Part of this trend is owing to Asian subsidies for capital-intensive businesses, but the American corporate tax system also bears a great deal of the blame. The Tax Foundation wrote in a March 2022 study:

> To understand how the tax system disadvantages investment in physical capital, one must understand depreciation. Economically, depreciation is the way an asset declines in value over time as it wears out or becomes obsolete—but in the tax system, depreciation describes how a taxpayer can deduct investment costs over time. While most business costs, such as utility bills or wages and salaries, are immediately deducted when they are incurred, business costs associated with physical capital are not immediately deducted. Instead, businesses must follow recovery periods set by lawmakers, indicating how many years over which deductions must be spread.

> Just as justice delayed is justice denied, a deduction delayed is a deduction denied, or at least, devalued. We can see why because a dollar of deductions 10 years from now is not as valuable as a dollar of deductions today. Over time, infla-

tion and the time value of money reduce the real value of deferred deductions. When inflation is zero, the real-time value of money (a normal real return on capital of about 3 percent) is the only source of erosion. When inflation is present, the erosion is more severe. The recent increase in inflation makes the bias worse, and the need to resolve it even more urgent.

Recovery periods vary significantly across asset classes. Structures, or buildings, must be spread out over the longest amount of time: residential structures over 27.5 years, and commercial structures over 39 years. Companies must also spread their deductions for long-lived structures in equal increments, but for short-lived assets, such as various types of equipment, they can deduct a larger part of the costs in earlier years.

The ideal tax treatment of physical capital costs is full expensing, when they are deducted the year the investments are made. Immediately deducting costs ensures the value of the deductions is not eroded. The longer deductions are spread (and the higher the inflation rate), the worse for industry.[10]

Policy conclusion: Corporate taxation requires a radical reform to allow full expensing of capital expenditures in the year they are made. As the Tax Foundation observes, this will eliminate the attrition of investment tax benefits through inflation and encourage investment in capital-intensive industries.

RESTORE FEDERAL R&D AND DRIVE INNOVATION THROUGH THE DEFENSE BUDGET AND THROUGH TAX INCENTIVES FOR CORPORATE LABORATORIES

The federal development budget consumed 1.5 percent of GDP at the peak of the Apollo Moonshot program in the early 1960s. That proportion has fallen to about 0.30 percent during the past several years, according to the

National Science Foundation. The federal research budget as a percentage of GDP has not changed much since the 1960s, because federal funds continue to flow to universities. Where manufacturing is concerned, the development budget is more important. That reflects federal support for building of prototypes of new technologies. (FIG. 11.)

Along with federal development funding, our capacity to deploy federal funds efficiently has shrunk. Dr. Henry Kressel, the former director of RCA Labs and a prominent technology investor, wrote in the journal *American Affairs*:

> America once had a few large, well-funded, and well-managed multidisciplinary corporate laboratories that housed some of the most brilliant technological researchers. They worked in environments where exceptionally creative people could innovate and see the fruits of their work translate into breakthrough products. . . .
>
> Such large, interdisciplinary corporate labs were the primary generators of new electronic and materials technologies. In fact, most of the basic innovations in computers, semiconductors, and software that enabled digital technology came out of the big U.S. corporate R&D organizations, which were formerly part of AT&T, General Electric, IBM, Xerox, RCA, and a few others. In addition, start-up companies that grew into giants such as Intel or Cisco initially leveraged technologies developed by the big companies or university laboratories. For example, Intel leveraged semiconductor technology from Bell Labs and Cisco originally leveraged digital communications technology developed with defense funding.[11]

Engineering departments are able to perform "evolutionary" technology development, which involves incrementally improving existing technologies or finding new uses for them. But "breakthrough innovations," Kressel states, require "very special environments where creative people have the freedom to follow their instincts and

FIGURE 11. FEDERAL R&D (ESPECIALLY DEVELOPMENT) SHRINKS AS SHARE OF GDP

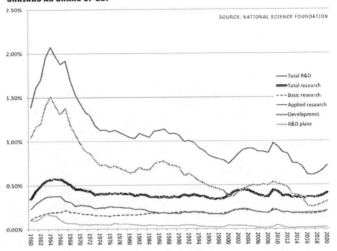

FIGURE 12. MANUFACTURING JOB OPENINGS

where management is focused on longer-term value creation."

The first and, by far, the largest and most productive of the corporate laboratories was AT&T Labs. AT&T had a monopoly on US telecommunications and systematically overcharged consumers for telephone service. Part of that subsidy financed its research facilities, which produced nine Nobel Prizes and 12,500 patents. AT&T Labs invented the transistor, the laser, the photovoltaic cell, and dozens of other elements of the digital economy. The breakup of the Bell system under a federal antitrust mandate reduced the cost of telephony for consumers, but it also removed the subsidy that supported AT&T's research efforts.

TRAIN A SKILLED WORKFORCE

The United States has a shortage of skilled labor. An unprecedented one million manufacturing job openings remained unfilled as of April 2022. (FIG.12.)

Fully 8 percent of all manufacturing jobs remain unfilled. The extraordinary rise in this number is without doubt related to the COVID-19 pandemic and the $6 trillion in subsidies for household incomes offered by the government in response. The labor force participation rate had not recovered to prepandemic levels as of May 2022, evidently because large numbers of workers chose to spend the subsidies rather than return to the workforce. But the overall decline in labor force participation accounts for just 1.6 million missing workers, while the gap in manufacturing alone is a million workers.

Many conservatives (and some liberals) view the decline in US manufacturing jobs as an important cause of declining living standards and social conditions, and they have proposed measures to restore manufacturing jobs for the benefit of American workers. The problem is more

FIGURE 13. MANUFACTURING VS ALL EMPLOYEES' HOURLY WAGES

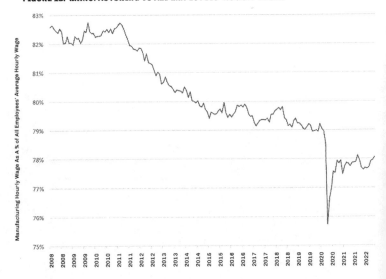

FIGURE 14. MANUFACTURING OUTPUT BY MANHOUR

complex: many Americans do not want the manufacturing jobs on offer.

That isn't surprising. Manufacturing wages have fallen relative to the average wage during the past fifteen years. In 2008, the average manufacturing hourly wage was 83 percent of the average hourly wage for all workers. By 2022, it had fallen to 78 percent of the average for all workers. (FIG. 13.) Manufacturing work is physically demanding and more dangerous than many other kinds of employment, and Americans are not paid enough to take up the manufacturing jobs on offer.

Manufacturing productivity (output per manhour), moreover, has declined since its peak in 2010. To put this in context: Output per manhour for US manufacturing workers doubled between 1993 and 2010, and then fell slightly during the next ten years. (FIG. 14.)

Manufacturing wages peaked in real terms in 1975 and have declined since then. The chart below adjusts the average hourly wage for manufacturing by the Consumer Price Index, as reported by the Bureau of Labor Statistics. The average hourly wage for US factor workers in 1947 was $1 an hour. It is now $25 an hour, but the Consumer Price Index has risen sixteen-fold, so the present $25 wage buys just $1.80 in 1947 dollars. In 1975 it bought $2 in 1947 dollars. The entire growth in hourly compensation since 1947 occurred in the years from 1947 to 1979. (FIG. 15)

What caused the decline in real hourly wages? It is noteworthy that the reversal of a thirty-year trend toward higher real manufacturing hourly wages preceded the appearance of substantial US trade deficits in manufactured goods and the offshoring of US production. The variable that tracks wage growth best over the long term is the change in the nation's capital stock.[12] A worker with a backhoe is more productive than a worker with a shovel. A manufacturing worker guiding a robot is more productive

FIGURE 15. MANUFACTURING HOURLY WAGES IN 1947 DOLLARS

**FIGURE 16. REAL MANUFACTURING WAGE GROWTH
VS CHANGE IN US CAPITAL STOCK**

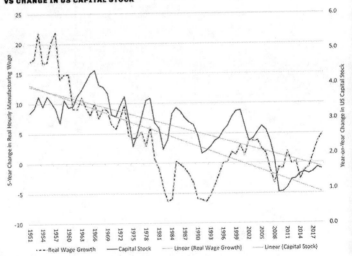

than a worker assembling products by hand. Capital intensity is the driver of productivity.

The chart in FIG. 16 shows the five-year change in real wages versus the annual change in the capital stock. The two variables trend together, and their relationship is intuitive. Many things affected the decline in real factory wages after 1975—notably, the oil price shock and subsequent inflation, but the long-term driver of real wages is the capital intensity of production.

The decline in capital stock growth also coincided with a gradual increase of imports vs. exports. This also tracks the decline in real wages. The damage to factory workers' incomes, we observe, was done a generation before China became a significant factor in world trade and an important source of US imports.

As we have seen, China played no role in the decline of factory wages starting in 1975. But the great import surge from China starting in the early 2000s coincided with the fastest decline in history of US manufacturing employment. (FIG. 17.)

Labor compensation depends on productivity. The average German autoworker earned $67.14 in 2021, versus US autoworker compensation of $33.77 per hour, yet German automakers are highly profitable.

It is possible to divide up the pie differently between wages and profits, and reward workers by penalizing shareholders. But, as we saw above, the weighted average cost of capital for the US manufacturing industry is roughly in line with other parts of the corporate world. If government action assigned a higher share of revenues to labor compensation and a lower share to profits, capital would flow out of the manufacturing sector to more profitable sectors of the economy.

It is also possible to increase the price of manufactured goods by imposing restrictions on imports. That was the

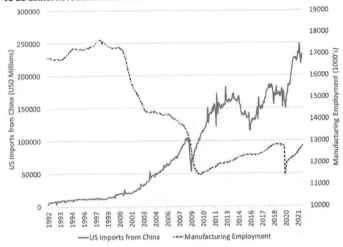

FIGURE 17. IMPORTS FROM CHINA VS US MANUFACTURING EMPLOYMENT

object of the United States-Mexico-Canada Trade Act of July 2020. A fact sheet published by the United States Trade Representative states,

> This deal uses trade rules to drive higher wages by requiring that 40–45 percent of auto content be made by workers earning at least $16 per hour. The rules will support better jobs for United States producers and workers by requiring that a significant portion of vehicle content be made with high-wage labor [and] ensure that United States producers and workers are able to compete on an even playing field. [13]

That is a transfer of income from purchasers of cars to makers of cars. It is possible to do this in selected industries, but the application of this approach to a broad range of manufactured products would increase prices substantially. An arbitrary group of workers (those employed in protected industries) would be subsidized by an arbitrary group of citizens (purchasers of the products of those industries).

Declining productivity has one explanation: As US manufacturing shrank relative to the size of the economy, relatively unproductive legacy industries remained. These considerations lead to a remarkable conclusion: The United States has the wrong sort of manufacturing industry and the wrong sort of manufacturing workforce. It requires new industries with high productivity growth and a highly skilled workforce able to assimilate new technologies.

AN APPRENTICESHIP SYSTEM ON THE GERMAN-SWISS-SCANDINAVIAN MODEL

Germany, Sweden, and Switzerland offer a model of industrial success in which a high-skilled and well-paid workforce supports industries that compete successfully with China and other Asian countries. Manufacturing comprises about a fifth of German GDP and a fourth of Chinese GDP, compared to a tenth of American GDP.

The German apprenticeship program embraces more than three hundred skills and incorporates more than half of all Germans under the age of twenty-two. Training in industrial and service professions is rigorous, typically requiring three years of full-time work-study, which may be supplemented with an additional year of study to obtain a master's certificate.

We can't clone the European system, but we can draw an obvious lesson from it. Governments need to provide an alternative to overpriced and often useless university educations, and industry needs to provide curricula and teachers. There is no need to wait for the federal government to get its act together. Several states currently preside over systems of universities and community colleges that waste the time and tuition of many of their students. With a public-private partnership, the leading state university systems could be transformed rapidly into sources of skills for industrial excellence. To provide Fourth Industrial

FIGURE 18. SCIENCE AND ENGINEERING
BACHELOR'S DEGREES PER YEAR

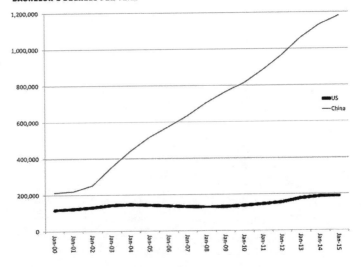

Revolution skills, the state university system needs private industry to identify the kind of skills it wants in employees, and to provide curricula, instructors, and—most important—work-study opportunities to help students pay for their education while they learn. Unlike the European system, which separates students into academic and vocational tracks, America can award two-year degrees for training in industrial skills, while giving students the option to pursue a four-year bachelor's degree if they so choose.

DIRECT TERTIARY EDUCATION SUBSIDIES TO ENGINEERING

The United States has a comparative lack of trained engineers. As of 2016, China graduated six times as many engineering bachelor's degrees as the United States, according to the National Science Foundation. About a third of Chinese undergraduates study engineering, compared to 7 percent of American undergraduates. (FIG. 18.)

America needs a new National Defense Education Act. According to the official history of the US House of Representatives, "National Defense Education Act (NDEA) was passed in 1958 in response to Soviet acceleration of the space race with the launch of the satellite Sputnik. The law provided federal funding to 'insure trained manpower of sufficient quality and quantity to meet the national defense needs of the United States.' In addition to fellowships and loans to students, the legislation bolstered education in the areas of science, mathematics, and modern foreign languages."[14] Such legislation can be enacted today.

INVEST IN THE FUTURE, NOT THE PAST

With few exceptions, industries that moved to China won't come home. Henry Kressel wrote in the *Asia Times:*

> An example of a failed attempt to reverse offshoring is instructive: solar cell panels for electricity generation. A US company named Suniva attempted to compete with Chinese vendors once they established themselves in the 2010 period.
>
> In parallel with efforts in the US and Germany, the Chinese government decided to make solar energy production a national priority. With imported technology and massive government financial support, large production companies emerged that quickly become international suppliers at ever-decreasing prices. The focus was on cutting costs.
>
> The strategy was based on building vertically integrated companies producing all the key elements of panels from silicon to glass frames to deliver the lowest cost panels while maintaining quality.
>
> It became a $30 billion industry as, one by one, international competitors went out of business—unable to compete on price.

Suniva, a US company with excellent technology, attempted to compete but found that its domestic suppliers of components had disappeared. Suniva had to import from China its key supplies. There was no profit margin. The company eventually closed despite the imposition of import duties by the US government.[15]

China has fostered a manufacturing ecosystem that provides manufacturers with multiple suppliers, an extensive supply of skilled labor, and engineering skills. An example is the enormous Huaqiangbei electronics market in Shenzhen, China's Silicon Valley. The multistory electronics mall hosts 38,000 businesses that sell supplies to the city's electronics industry.

Apple CEO Tim Cook, whose flagship iPhone products are mainly assembled in China, said:

> There's a confusion about China. The popular conception is that companies come to China because of low labor cost. I'm not sure what part of China they go to, but the truth is China stopped being the low-labor-cost country many years ago. And that is not the reason to come to China from a supply point of view. The reason is because of the skill, and the quantity of skill in one location and the type of skill it is.

> The products we do require really advanced tooling, and the precision that you have to have, the tooling and working with the materials that we do are state of the art. And the tooling skill is very deep here. In the U.S., you could have a meeting of tooling engineers and I'm not sure we could fill the room. In China, you could fill multiple football fields.[16]

These examples illustrate the difficulty of reshoring established big industries. Without deep infrastructure, reshored enterprises cannot compete. Rebuilding such infrastructure is costly and there is little private capital appetite for such programs.

The industries of the future, though, well may flourish in the United States. A leading example is Tesla, the world's leading manufacturer of electric vehicles, which developed its production process in the United States and will continue to manufacture in the United States despite its overseas expansion. Frontier technologies open even greater opportunities in manufacturing industry.

Although the United States only produces about 12 percent of the world's semiconductors, down from 37 percent in 1990, a disproportionate share of semiconductor intellectual property is held in the United States. Revolutionary changes in chip design and construction may make obsolete a large part of the world's semiconductor fabrication capacity. Taiwanese and South Korean companies have made enormous investments in the expensive process of producing chips with transistors as small as three nanometers. New technologies, including advanced packaging, which "stack" transistors in three dimensions, may achieve the same degree of miniaturization, speed, and energy efficiency at considerably less cost. Artificial intelligence promises to speed chip design and increase fabrication efficiency.

These technologies are at an early phase of development. A 2021 McKinsey report concludes,

> Artificial intelligence/machine learning (AI/ML) has the potential to generate huge business value for semiconductor companies at every step of their operations, from research and chip design to production through sales. But our recent survey of semiconductor-device makers shows that only about 30 percent of respondents stated that they are already generating value through AI/ML.[17]

The next generation of robotics may employ artificial intelligence and high-speed broadband to enable machines to self-program. That opens the possibility of flexible manufacturing on a mass scale, allowing manufacturers to create their own supply chains for industrial parts as needed.

Henry Kressel explains:

> Flexible high-tech manufacturing relies on the creative application of IT through the use of massive timely data and artificial intelligence, robotics, sensor deployment and ubiquitous communications to link the factors bearing on manufacturing. Such plants with suitable interlinked sensors are well suited for a high level of in-process quality control and documentation. . . .

> The model that has pioneered this concept is the chip industry. We are benefiting from continuous and remarkable innovations in device manufacturing since the 1960s when a single silicon switching transistor (the core device in computing) cost US$5. Today, built with a totally different technology, a silicon chip the size of a fingernail containing 1 billion interconnected transistors sells for the same price.

> This is the result of amazing innovations (many in the US) in optics, robotics, chemistry and software to integrate the various parts of the production process. Workers are highly trained technicians able to control remotely very complex and costly machines. In fact, robots do the process work because the cleanliness levels are so high that humans cannot come in contact with the production in process lest they contribute dust particles.[18]

Flexible manufacturing to a great extent can offset China's advantage in deep industrial ecosystems. Programmable robots guided by artificial intelligence and 3D printing will allow small and agile manufacturers to create a wide variety of electronic and mechanical parts to order, and a small but well-trained technical workforce can substitute for skilled labor that may be in short supply.

The requirements of national defense have always been the great driver of American innovation. Every component of the digital age, including fast and inexpensive integrated circuits, plasma and LED displays, the GUI interface, optical networks, and the internet began with a grant by the Defense Advanced Projects Research Agency to a corporate laboratory.

CMOS chip manufacturing began with DARPA grants to Fairchild Semiconductor and RCA Labs, originally with the aim of enabling weather forecasting in military aircraft. It became the standard process for chip manufacturing, used for 99 percent of integrated circuit chips by 2011. RCA commercialized the process in the late 1960s (when Dr. Henry Kressel was the corporate vice president in charge of RCA Labs). With a DARPA grant initially intended to improve nighttime illumination of battlefields, RCA Labs perfected the semiconductor laser as a low-power light source for optical devices. Vast increases in data transmission through optical networks became possible, launching several new industries including cable television and, eventually, the internet. The Graphical User Interface (GUI) was developed with a DARPA grant to Xerox Laboratories in Palo Alto. This made possible a new kind of software as well as the computer mouse, invented by Douglas Engelbart at the Stanford Research Institute.

Every invention of the digital age, in fact, has these elements in common:

1. All were invented in the United States.

2. All began with government funding for basic research.

3. All were developed at a corporate laboratory that brought together scientists, engineers, and produc-

tion personnel who worked together to determine the viability of the invention.

4. All began with an objective unrelated to the ultimate product.

5. All were commercialized with private capital, although the basic research was funded by the government.

The term "public-private partnership" was not in vogue at the peak of the Digital Revolution, but that is the origin of core industries of the digital age: personal computers, flat-panel displays, optical networks, consumer and business software, and the internet.

The Digital Revolution teaches us one basic lesson: *Industrial policy will fail if it directs public capital to specific, established technologies.* None of the definitive technologies that made the Digital Revolution were understood except in embryo before DARPA funded them. Creative engineers and scientists discovered technologies that no one could have imagined prior to their discovery and launched multi-hundred-billion-dollar industries that no one could have envisioned before the technologies became available.

That is why a defense driver is the key to industrial policy. For better or worse, the exigencies of defense push research to the frontiers of physics and require true innovations—in artificial intelligence, computation, Integrated Circuit design and manufacturing, air- and hydrodynamics, materials science, and other fields. We cannot predict in advance what our most creative (and sometimes eccentric) engineers and scientists will discover. We require a modicum of faith in American creativity to embrace the unknown unknowns.

We do not know which defense technologies will be decisive. But we do know that most expensive items in our defense hardware budget, stealth aircraft and aircraft carriers, are mature technologies that can be defeated by existing technology, or are likely to be defeated by soon-to-be-developed technology. The total cost of the F-35 program alone is likely to be $1.7 trillion over the life of the program.[19] In theory, drone swarms guided by high-speed broadband and controlled by artificial intelligence can accomplish what fighter aircraft now do much more effectively and at a fraction of the cost. Airframes can achieve twice the speed of the fastest manned fighter aircraft, but the human body cannot tolerate the stress. Nontrivial problems in communication, computation, and data security limit the practicality of such weapons systems for the time being.

A seismic shift in defense priorities is required both to secure the American homeland against foreign threats and to drive the innovation required to place America at the forefront of the creation of new industries. As noted above, the federal development budget is now just 0.3 percent of GDP, compared to 1.5 percent of GDP at the peak of the Apollo program in the 1960s and close to 1 percent during the late 1970s and 1980s. To restore funding levels to a proportion comparable to the 1970s and 1980s would require an additional expenditure of $150 billion to $200 billion a year.

The defense budget should focus on future war-fighting technologies such as

1. Space-based missile defense.
2. Directed-energy antimissile and other weapons.
3. Drone swarms.
4. Submarine detection (including quantum computing applications).
5. Quantum cryptography.
6. Hardening of satellites against possible attack.
7. Hypersonic vehicles (offense and defense).

Key to success is the revival of the corporate laboratory system, as noted above. An important obstacle to overcome is the reluctance of America's Big Tech companies to work for national defense. That is not a trivial problem, but it can be addressed by the right combination of tax incentives and disincentives as well as defense scholarship programs for university students.

CONCLUSION

Economic theory is baffled by innovation. There are many attempts to incorporate innovation into the conventional model in which given capital and labor inputs produce a given amount of output. Paul Romer won the Nobel Prize in 2018 for his efforts to add innovation to the model, by including R&D as a multiplier of capital and labor inputs. But innovation never proceeds in such an orderly fashion. An invention that may have accounted for the single largest increase in productivity in economic history, the domestication of the cat for rodent control, required de minimis inputs of capital (a bowl of milk) and labor ("Here, kitty-kitty"). By definition, it is impossible to identify fundamental innovations ex ante. We know what they are when we see them, and not before.

War is the father of all things, said Heraclitus. He meant something different by the phrase, but it remains apt: We stand on the threshold of changes in economic behavior which we could not have imagined a generation ago and which we can barely imagine now. There is no field of economic activity that will not be transformed by the combination of high-speed broadband and artificial intelligence. AI will replace a great deal of dull, mind-deadening, low-paid, repetitive work: Driving vehicles, sorting packages in warehouses, tightening bolts on an assembly line, transferring containers from ship to truck, taking inventory, delivering fertilizer to plants, and so forth. But the prospect of boundless prosperity and freedom from drudgery will not be sufficient to motivate us to embrace innovation and transform our lives for the better. We will undertake and adapt to innovation when the exigencies of defense compel us to do so.

The railroads transformed America and became the carrier technology that made possible America's leap into industrial leadership in the late nineteenth century, but it took a civil war to create a national consensus around federal subsidies to build railroads. Computation, jet aviation, rocketry, and a dozen other technologies defined the great economic expansion after World War II, but it took a war to build the first computers. All the elements of the Digital Age were visible in embryo form when a Texas Instruments engineer invented the integrated circuit in 1958, but it took another twenty years and the exigencies of the Cold War for the digital revolution to begin in earnest.

Innovation on behalf of national defense does not necessarily lead to war. On the contrary, the great innovations of the late 1970s and early 1980s prevented hot war with the Soviet Union, by persuading Moscow that it could not keep up with America's new weapons systems.

We do not need to prepare for a global supply chain disruption like the one created by the COVID-19 pandemic. But our economy should be able to adapt to unforeseen contingencies. The key to industrial security is a highly skilled workforce and a corporate manufacturing culture. We can't invest in advance for every possible contingency, but if we have the skills and the robotics, we can quickly build up capacity where we might require it.

We should take to heart the observation of Professor Edmund Phelps, the 2005 Nobel Laureate in economics:

> New technologies are not costlessly absorbed into the market economy, so the link from invention to innovation

is not prompt or reliable. It takes a creative entrepreneur to solve the problems in developing and marketing an innovation; it takes Nelson-Phelps managers to solve the problem of evaluating the innovation's likely gains, if any; it takes the of type of consumers described by Amar Bhidé to solve the problem of evaluating the gains, if any, of bringing an innovation home; and it takes financiers who can do better than choosing randomly in deciding which entrepreneurs to back. In sum, it takes a whole village for an innovation to be developed, launched and adopted.

We simply have to cut the Gordian Knot, or rather, seven Gordian Knots:

1. To establish tax and regulatory conditions that foster manufacturing, as opposed to the present system that favors capital-light industries.

2. To shift the defense budget away from costly, obsolete weapons systems to support for innovative weapons that push the frontier of physics and computation.

3. To subsidize a very few critical industries (for example semiconductors) whose onshore operation is vital to national defense and economic security.

4. To foster innovation at the frontier of science—first of all in the service of national defense, but by extension in the interest of long-term productivity and growth.

5. To protect industry from harmful monopolies, in this case Big Tech, which stifles innovation and diverts capital away from essential industries.

6. To shift educational subsidies away from elite institutions that train financiers and functionaries, to an apprenticeship system that trains skilled workers for high-tech industry.

7. To require a school curriculum that emphasizes literacy and numeracy in preparation for skilled jobs and engineering studies.

Why has this not been accomplished before? Entrenched monopolies are powerful. The Big Tech lobby has enormous influence in the writing of tax legislation. The defense contractors have an enormous, vested interest in legacy weapons systems and little incentive to allocate their R&D budget to "unknown unknowns." The educational system is perhaps the most powerful monopoly of all. Together, our vested interests and entrenched monopolies have suffocated innovation and forced the bulk of our industrial capacity into other venues. As matters stand, America is headed for second-rate status, like Great Britain before us. This is perhaps our last opportunity to get back on track.

ABOUT THE AUTHOR

David P. Goldman is a Washington Fellow at the Claremont Institute's Center for the American Way of Life, as well as the president of Macrostrategy LLC. He writes the "Spengler" column for *Asia Times Online* and the "Spengler" blog at *PJ Media*, and is the author of several books, including, *You Will Be Assimilated: China's Plan to Sino-Form the World* (Bombardier Books), and *How Civilizations Die (and Why Islam is Dying Too)* (Regnery). His previous book in this series is *Provocations #2: How America Can Lose the Fourth Industrial Revolution* (Claremont Press).

ENDNOTES

1. "Red Ink: Estimating Chinese Industrial Policy Spending in Comparative Perspective," Center for Strategic & International Studies, May 23, 2022, https://www.csis.org/analysis/red-ink-estimating-chinese-industrial-policy-spending-comparative-perspective; Rob Garver, "Report: China Spends Billions of Dollars to Subsidize Favored Companies," VOA, May 24, 2022, https://www.voanews.com/a/report-china-spends-billions-of-dollars-to-subsidize-favored-companies-/6587314.html.

2. Chuin-Wei Yap, "State Support Helped Fuel Huawei's Global Rise," *Wall Street Journal*, December 25, 2019, https://www.wsj.com/articles/state-support-helped-fuel-huaweis-global-rise-11577280736.

3. "2.1 Million Manufacturing Jobs Could Go Unfilled by 2030," National Association of Manufacturing, May 4, 2021, https://www.nam.org/2-1-million-manufacturing-jobs-could-go-unfilled-by-2030-13743/.

4. See Justin Lin, "China Must Lead the Next Industrial Revolution," *Asia Times*, October 15, 2021, https://asiatimes.com/2021/10/china-must-lead-the-new-industrial-revolution/.

5. Tianlei Huang and Nicholas R. Lardy, "Foreign Corporates Investing in China Surged in 2021," Peterson Institute for International Economics, March 29, 2022, https://www.piie.com/blogs/realtime-economic-issues-watch/foreign-corporates-investing-china-surged-2021.

6. Michael Zezas et al., "Navigating 'Slowbalization' and the Multipolar World," Morgan Stanley Research, May 18, 2022.

7. Drew Fitzgerald, "White House Considers Broad Federal Intervention to Secure 5G Future," *Wall Street Journal*,

June 15, 2020, https://www.wsj.com/articles/white-house-federal-intervention-5g-huawei-china-nokia-trump-cisco-11593099054?mod=tech_lead_pos3.

8. US Congress, House of Representatives, Subcommittee on Antitrust, Commercial and Administrative Law of the Committee on the Judiciary, Investigation of Competition in Digital Markets, 116TH Congress, 2020, 6–7. See also David P. Goldman, "China's Attempt to Avoid the American Tech Monopoly Trap," *American Affairs* 5, no. 2 (Summer 2021).

9. Wikipedia, s.v. "Capital Intensity," last modified December 19, 2022, 15:34, https://en.wikipedia.org/wiki/Capital_intensity.

10. Erica York et al., "Taxes, Tariffs, and Industrial Policy: How the U.S. Tax Code Fails Manufacturing," Tax Foundation, March 2022, https://taxfoundation.org/us-manufacturing-tax-industrial-policy/.

11. Henry Kressel, "Edison's Legacy: Industrial Laboratories and Innovation," *American Affairs* 1, no. 4 (Winter 2017).

12. Robert C. Feenstra, Robert Inklaar, and Marcel P. Timmer, "The Next Generation of the Penn World Table," *American Economic Review* 105, no. 10 (2015): 3150–82, http://www.rug.nl/ggdc/. Retrieved from fred.stlouis.org, https://fred.stlouisfed.org/series/RKNANPUSA666NRUG#0.

13. "United States–Mexico–Canada Trade Fact Sheet: Rebalancing Trade to Support Manufacturing," Office of the United States Trade Representative, https://ustr.gov/trade-agreements/free-trade-agreements/united-states-mexico-canada-agreement/fact-sheets/rebalancing.

14. Unites States House of Representatives, https://history.house.gov/HouseRecord/Detail/15032436195.

15. Henry Kressel, "Winners and Losers in the Global Supply Chain," *Asia Times*, June 23, 2022, https://asiatimes.com/2022/06/winners-and-losers-in-the-global-supply-chain/.

16. Glenn Leibowitz, "Apple CEO Tim Cook: This Is the No. 1 Reason We Make iPhones in China (It's Not What You Think)," *Inc.com*, April 15, 2022, https://www.inc.com/glenn-leibowitz/apple-ceo-tim-cook-this-is-number-1-reason-we-make-iphones-in-china-its-not-what-you-think.html.

17. Sebastian Göke, Kevin Staight, and Rutger Vrijen, "Scaling AI in the Sector That Enables It: Lessons for Semiconductor-Device Makers," McKinsey & Company, April 2, 2021, https://www.mckinsey.com/industries/semiconductors/our-insights/scaling-ai-in-the-sector-that-enables-it-lessons-for-semiconductor-device-makers.

18. Henry Kressel, "Flexible High Tech Manufacturing is the Future," *Asia Times*, May 12, 2020, https://asiatimes.com/2020/05/flexible-high-tech-manufacturing-is-the-future/.

19. Charles P. Pierce, "This Country Is Spending $1.7 Trillion on Planes That Don't Work," *Esquire*, February 25, 2021, https://www.esquire.com/news-politics/politics/a35631305/f-35-doesnt-work-1-7-trillion-dollars/.

Made in the USA
Columbia, SC
15 August 2023

21612694R00033